35 Days
— & —
35 Ways

My Journal and My Journey

DOVIE LANNS

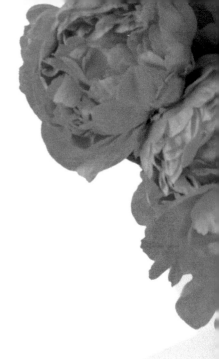

Published by Dovie L. Lanns
Produced by Create and Blossom Studios
www.createandblossomstudios.com
ISBN: 978-1-945304-88-0

Printed in the United States of America

Presented to

_____.

35 Days & 35 Ways

With today's busy lifestyles and many uncertainties from the world's many distractions, it is easy to get so wrapped up in life and lose focus on what's really important.

This journal contains 35 powerful messages to help you get through your day. It will help bring peace and calmness back into your life. By the end of this journal, you will have 35 things you are grateful for and 35 acts of kindness you've purposely shown someone else.
Let's start your journey today!

Happy Monday!!

Today is "Mindset Monday" Today is what you make it! You control your day! With God's Grace and Mercy, He woke you up in your right mind this morning! Someone, somewhere, did not make it, but you did. Yesterday is gone. Today is here with new grace and new mercies!

While everyone else is saying, "Oh my gosh, it's Monday," or "I hate Mondays," you say, " Bless the Lord for My Marvelous Monday. He woke me up in my right mind with renewed grace and mercy! Today is going to be a GREAT Day" Today, I pray that your day is filled with many great blessings. I pray for favor, healing, and peace over you today!

Monday:_____

How are you going to apply this message in your life today?

_____
_____
_____
_____
_____
_____
_____
_____
_____
_____
_____
_____
_____
_____
_____
_____
_____

Happy Tuesday!!

Today is "Triple T's Tuesday" (Time, Talk, & Thought). As I always say, we dictate our day. We decide what we entertain during our day. We set the mood for our day! Here are three important things to consider when setting the tone for your day. 1. How do you spend your TIME? 2. What do you TALK about? 3. What do you THINK about? First, spend some time with God in the morning, and set your tone for the day. Pray, meditate, read His Word, and most importantly, give Him thanks for waking you up to see another day. Secondly, be mindful of who you allow in your space and what they bring into it. One wrong conversation can change the entire course of your day. We have so much to be grateful for, so change how you speak. Life and death are in the power of the tongue. Do not complain, be grateful for where you are and what you have. Today, I challenge you to counter every complaint with a blessing. Lastly, as a man thinketh, so is he, so guard your thoughts, meditate on the good. Meditate on ALL that God has done for you, including waking you up to see another blessed day. What we think eventually becomes a reality. I pray that your day is filled with peace, joy, and God's unwavering Favor! I pray you have the courage, strength, and boldness to step out and do whatever dream or vision God has put in your heart. I pray that God blesses you beyond your wildest dreams.

Tuesday:_____

How are you going to apply this message in your life today?

_____
_____
_____
_____
_____
_____
_____
_____
_____
_____
_____
_____
_____
_____
_____
_____
_____
_____

Happy Wednesday!!

Today is "Why-Not Wednesday" Do not get discouraged because something did not quite work out the way you planned, everything is working out in your Favor. Sometimes it may not even make sense to you but trust and believe God hand is in it. When that door shuts or that thing did not go according to plan; just look at it as God was protecting you from something. He redirected you. So just take a step back, close your eyes, take a deep breath, and trust God with ALL your heart and soul. He has something better planned! Just know without a shadow of a doubt that he wants you to WIN! *The Lord is my light and salvation, whom shall I fear? The Lord is the strength of my life; whom shall I be afraid? (Psalms 27:1). Peace I leave with you, my peace I give unto you: not as the world giveth, give I unto you. Let not your heart be troubled, neither let it be afraid. (John 14:27)* Let's Praise Him, let's rejoice!! We are WINNERS! We are VICTORIOUS! We are MIGHTY and POWERFUL! Nothing can stop you! Nothing can break you! Because God is in you! I pray your day be filled with peace, joy, and divine purpose! I pray that every single thing that you breathe on and every single thing that you touch have Favor from God and from man.

Wednesday:_____

How are you going to apply this message in your life today?

_____
_____
_____
_____
_____
_____
_____
_____
_____
_____
_____
_____
_____
_____
_____
_____
_____

Happy Thursday!!

Today is "Thankful Thursday." First things first! If you are reading this message, give God thanks. Thank Him for waking you up to see another blessed day! Today is a new day! New Grace! New Mercy! New rested mind! God reset you! He gave you new life, & new breath! So thank Him for t! Be thankful and grateful for friendships and relationships, whether they are good or they have gone bad. Thank Him regardless. Sometimes losing someone we thought was upposed to be in our day-to-day lives can be tough. But God aw otherwise, so trust him in the process. Trust me; you will thank him later. Sometimes he only allows you to see or understand certain things because we tend to get in the way of His work, and we always mess things up for some reason. So He keeps us blinded when He's doing His work for a reason. "Don't be anxious about anything, but in every situation, by prayer and petition, with thanksgiving, present your requests to God. And the peace of God, which ranscends all understanding, will guard your heart and your minds in Christ Jesus." (Philippians 4:6) Today, I challenge you to give thanks and tell at least five people thank you for whatever reason. Stop throughout your day and tell God hank you because you still have your limbs, your vision, and your touch; even if you're not feeling well today, thank Him anyway because you're still alive. He can heal your body. All you have to do is trust Him and believe.

*Thursday:*_____

How are you going to apply this message in your life today?

_____
_____
_____
_____
_____
_____
_____
_____
_____
_____
_____
_____
_____
_____
_____
_____
_____
_____

Happy Friday!!

Let's rejoice!! Today is "Fight Flesh Friday" Today when a situation arises, I challenge you to think before you speak. Sometimes our flesh and anger makes us say and do hurtful things that we can not take back. Saying "I'm sorry" does not always work because those hurtful words are already out and cutting someone. So today, if you get into a situation, whether it is with someone close to you or a perfect stranger. Fight your flesh and respond with kindness or simply walk away.

Also, if you blatantly know you are about to do or say something on purpose that you know you should not, I ask that you fight the flesh. Do not allow a small situation to interfere with what God has in store for you because His plans are way bigger. Stay humbled, stay focused, keep your eyes on the prize. *"Those who are dominated by the sinful nature think about sinful things, but those who are controlled by the Holy Spirit think about things that please the Spirit. So letting your sinful nature control your mind leads to death. But letting the Spirit control your mind leads to life and peace." (Romans 8:5-6)* I pray you have a Fabulous Friday and an amazing purpose filled weekend!!

Friday:_____

How are you going to apply this message in your life today?

_____
_____
_____
_____
_____
_____
_____
_____
_____
_____
_____
_____
_____
_____
_____
_____

Grateful Saturday

List 5 things you are grateful for & why.

1

2

3

4

5

Sunday

List 5 acts of kindness that you will purposely do for someone this week.

1	

2	

3	

4	

5	

Happy Monday!!

Today is "Unapologetic Monday." Today is the day we will start believing, accepting, and owning EVERYTHING GOD has for us and EVERYTHING GOD called us to be. Today, we are going to start doing that unapologetically. We are not going to apologize for our blessings. We all have asked God to bless us with certain things, but when the blessings start to roll in, we tend to tuck our tails or dim the light on our blessings because we do not want to offend or intimidate someone. Well, that stops today!! If someone is intimidated by you or your blessings and success or if someone gets offended when you share your blessings, they either need to step their game up or find another table to eat at. We are in the season of being everything God called us to be, and we will not apologize for it. Those types of people are called haters. They secretly do not want you to see you win. We are going to start today by owning who we are (A Child of the Most High). We are going to start accepting and owning our gifts and blessings, and we are doing it unapologetically. Repeat after me, "I will NOT apologize to anyone for God's great Favor, and I will NOT allow anyone to make me feel less because they can not see more for themselves. Walk in your Favor! Walk in your Peace! Walk in your Blessings!

Monday:_____

How are you going to apply this message in your life today?

_____

_____

_____

_____

_____

_____

_____

_____

_____

_____

_____

_____

_____

_____

_____

_____

Happy Tuesday!!

oday is "Talk It Up Tuesday." Today, let's talk it up!! Whatever ur heart desires, talk it up. Whether it is a better job, a stronger relationship, finances, health, a new home, a new car, etc. Whatever it may be! It is yours to have! All you have to do is pray, ask, and believe! But you MUST have Faith! Start by hanking Him for what you already have, then start thanking Iim and Praising Him in advance for what you want. Remain humble and patient! "Death and life are in the power of the ongue, and those who love it will eat its fruit" (Proverbs 18:21). Ask, and it will be given to you; seek, and you will find; knock, d it will be opened to you. For everyone who asks receives, and ie who seeks finds, and to him who knocks it will be opened"

(Matthew 7:7-8)

oray your Tuesday is as fabulous as you are! I pray your day is led with peace, joy, and love! I pray everything you touch and breathe on has *favor* with God and with man!

19

Tuesday:_____

How are you going to apply this message in your life today?

_____
_____
_____
_____
_____
_____
_____
_____
_____
_____
_____
_____
_____
_____
_____
_____

Happy Wednesday!!

Today is "Work it out Wednesday" Whatever it is you have been struggling with over the past couple of days, weeks, or maybe even onths, it is time to STOP! Whether it is a relationship, friendship, an ed apology, forgiveness, debt, a decision that needs to be made, your ealth, etc... It is now time to stop! Stop giving that thing power! Stop ving that thing control! Anytime you allow something or someone to disturb your peace and disturb your energy, or it is causing tress/anxiety in your life, you have given that person or thing total ontrol over your life. Don't ever give anything or anyone that much itrol over your life. Put your head down, keep your shoulders square d strong, and run into that thing head-on. Charge it with everything u have inside of you. Do not run from it, do not avoid it because that eaky little thing will always find its way back somehow. Work it out at the source! Get rid of it!

u have to take the first step. You and only you control you and your eace. Sometimes, it may not be easy, but I guarantee you it will be orth it. There is nothing greater than peace of mind. So I challenge ou today to face that mountain. Pray and ask God for courage and ength! Activate your faith and climb that mountain with everything ou have in you. I pray you will find the courage and the strength to face any situation in your life today. I pray you will put on the full rmor of God and fight for your peace. I pray everything you have en struggling with or going through has been defeated in the Mighty Name of Jesus! WORK IT OUT!! You are not alone. God is with you every step of the way.

Wednesday:_____

How are you going to apply this message in your life today?

_____
_____
_____
_____
_____
_____
_____
_____
_____
_____
_____
_____
_____
_____

Happy Thursday!!

Today is "Throwback Thursday" As we all know this is well known around social media when people post old pictures of themselves or their family. Today, you are going to flip it. You are going to think about who you used to be, the things you use to do, the situations you have put yourselves in, or even situations that were a test and process from God himself. You are going to take a quick moment and just look back at how far you have come. Take a moment to reflect on ALL the situations God has brought you out of. Take a moment to reflect on that sickness you had in your body and you know without a shadow of a doubt that it was God that brought you out and saw you through. It was God that kept you standing strong. It was God that spared your life in that car accident. It was God that kept a hedge of protection around your children and kept them safe. It was God that sent that unexpected check in the mail. It was God that told the doctors they don't see the same diagnosis they saw before. It was God that gave you that credit on that bill. It was God that told the cashier to give you that extra discount. It was and still is ALLL God!!! Now please do not stay in the past too long because sometimes that moment of comfort will take you back because we are naturally drawn to what's comfortable and familiar.

And that makes us feel safe. Today we're only reflecting on His goodness and His mercies!! Think about this: When you are driving in your car, that rearview mirror is so small compared to that large windshield. That rearview mirror isn't designed for you to look at it for a long period of time, it is designed for you to glimpse back and immediately turn your focus to the big windshield in front of you. If you stare into that tiny rearview mirror too long, you're going to crash. The windshield allows you to see far ahead of you. Just like life, take a quick look back to see how far God has brought you. Look ahead to the big limitless future you have ahead of you. I pray you have a wonderful day. May God continues to bless you and your family.

*Thursday:*_____

How are you going to apply this message in your life today?

_____

_____

_____

_____

_____

_____

_____

_____

_____

_____

_____

_____

_____

_____

_____

_____

Happy Friday!!

Affirmation Friday

Today is "I AM Friday" I AM GRATEFUL, I AM BLESSED, I AM WHOLE, I AM PEACEFUL, I AM LOVED, I AM BOLD, I AM COURAGEOUS, I AM GIVING, I AM THANKFUL, I AM JOYFUL, I AM FEARLESS, I AM STRONG, I AM FOCUSED, I AM GREAT, I AM WELL BALANCED, I AM EVERYTHING I SAY I AM.

Speak life into yourself today! Speak it with authority! I pray that your day is filled with everything your heart desires.

Friday: _____

How are you going to apply this message in your life today?

_____

_____

_____

_____

_____

_____

_____

_____

_____

_____

_____

_____

_____

_____

_____

_____

_____

_____

Grateful Saturday

List 5 things you are grateful for & why.

1

2

3

4

5

Sunday

List 5 acts of kindness that you will purposely do for someone this week.

1

2

3

4

5

Happy Monday!!

Today is "Motivation Monday". Today, I challenge you to take that leap of Faith and take that first step. While you are waiting on God to do that thing in your life, He is waiting for you to step out on Faith and make the first move. Trust Him! Go for it! Whatever it may be, make up your mind that you're going to go all in and trust God! So get up, get moving, and LET'S GOOO!! I pray your day is filled with peace, joy, and love. I pray God gives you the courage and strength to do whatever it is you desire as long as it is aligned with His Word!

*Monday:*_____

How are you going to apply this message in your life today?

_____

_____

_____

_____

_____

_____

_____

_____

_____

_____

_____

_____

_____

_____

_____

_____

_____

Happy Tuesday!!

Today is "Take Charge Tuesday". Today, I challenge you to take charge of your day. Own it! You took that leap of faith from yesterday's message and stepped out there to do that thing. Now today, let's own it! Take charge and push! The only person that can stop you or get in your way is you! Stop self-sabotaging yourself! Get out of your own way! Get out of your own head! God wants to see you prosper! God wants to see you win! Who do you think gave you the vision/dream in the first place? So today, you're going to rebuke any thought, any sign of fear that comes up.

YOU ARE VICTORIOUS!
YOU ARE A CHAMPION! YOU WILL WIN!

"For God has not given us a spirit of fear, but of power, and of love, and of a sound mind" 2 Timothy 1:7 I pray that your day is filled with courage and strength. I pray you to activate your faith and trust God with all your heart and soul. I pray that God gives you the wisdom, knowledge, and understanding of whatever that thing is that you're going after as long as it's aligned with His Word. I rebuke the spirit of fear and anxiety in the Mighty name of Jesus!

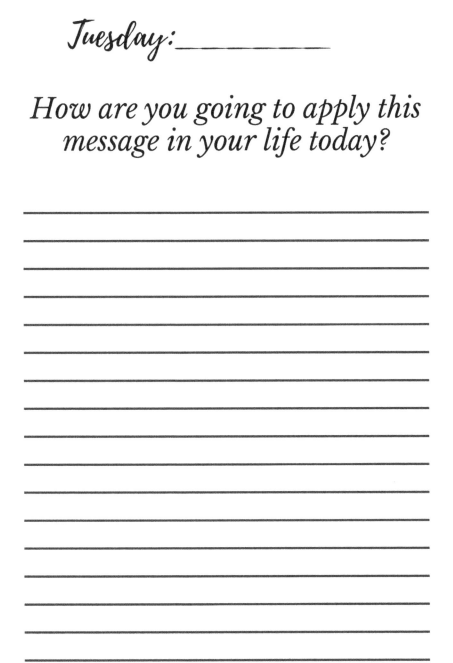

*Tuesday:*_____

How are you going to apply this message in your life today?

_____

_____

_____

_____

_____

_____

_____

_____

_____

_____

_____

_____

_____

_____

_____

_____

_____

_____

Happy Wednesday!!

Today is "Set Boundaries Wednesday." Today, we are going to talk about setting boundaries. The scripture says, "God is not a author of confusion, but of love, peace, and a sound mind." So with that being said, you must set boundaries for yourself to protect your peace. A boundary is a line that marks the limits an area; a dividing line. Some people you are going to deal with whether friends, coworkers, or family, do not know what a boundary is, or they do not respect yours. Yes, people make mistakes, and we want to be there for our family and friends but when you have someone constantly doing the same thing speaking the same way over and over again, it is no longer a mistake; it has become a lifestyle. Those are the ones for you have set boundaries for yourself. If you do not, before you know it, you will have prematurely planted yourself into their situation, and you have become their situation. Now you are worried and stressed by something that has nothing to do with you. Some may say, "God never turned His back on you," and they would be right. But God also gives us free will to live and make mistakes, and yes, He is always there to pick us right up. is ok to set a boundary and back off, but continue to pray for that person in hopes that they will turn to God with their troubles. So today, I challenge you to set boundaries for yourself. Say No! Guard your peace! The best anti-aging medication is peace and joy. I pray your day is filled with peace joy, and love.

Wednesday:_____

How are you going to apply this message in your life today?

_____

_____

_____

_____

_____

_____

_____

_____

_____

_____

_____

_____

_____

_____

_____

_____

_____

Happy Thursday!!

Today is "push Through Thursday" Yay!! Pat yourself on the back. You're almost there. You are on the way to completing another week. No matter how your week started off, God woke you up every day this week with new Grace, new Mercy, new Strength, and new Courage. He has given you another day to push through and keep going. It does not matter how your week started. You are going to finish. So I challenge you to get up today, put on your whole armor of God, and fight. Push your way through whatever it was trying to hold you back from your goal this week. God has dealt everyone a measure of Faith. Activate your Faith today, trust God and PUSH until you break through that thing! Don't give up now! You're almost there!

"And let us not grow weary while doing good, for in due season we shall reap if we do not lose heart" Galatians 6:9

I pray that God gives you the strength and courage to handle anything that comes up against you. God said, "no weapon formed against you shall prosper," and God CAN NOT lie. So He said it. You believe it with everything inside of you. I pray that your day is filled with peace, love, and joy.
In the Mighty Name of Jesus!

*Thursday:*_____

How are you going to apply this message in your life today?

_____

_____

_____

_____

_____

_____

_____

_____

_____

_____

_____

_____

_____

_____

_____

_____

Happy Friday!!

Let's celebrate another week in the books. Make the best of your day. Regardless of how this week has been for you, whether it was great or whether it was not so great, you still have a chance to turn it around in this one day. It is up to you. Are you feeling defeated or are you going to make up your mind that you are going to be victorious no matter what? Remember, you can not control what others do or say, but you can control how you respond and react. Anytime you are around an individual or someone mentions an individual's name and it changes your entire mood or day; That is called control!! Do not ever give someone else that much control over your life that the mention of their name disturbs your peace. Break that! Because that one thing changes your entire day, you and only you control your day. You make up your mind about which way it is going to go. I pray your day is filled with lots of love, peace, and happiness. Have an AMAZING weekend!!

*Friday:*_____

How are you going to apply this message in your life today?

_____
_____
_____
_____
_____
_____
_____
_____
_____
_____
_____
_____
_____
_____
_____
_____

Grateful Saturday

List 5 things you are grateful for & why.

1

2

3

4

5

Sunday

List 5 acts of kindness that you will purposely do for someone this week.

1

2

3

4

5

Happy Monday!!

Today is "Mind Over Matter Monday". Make up in your mind today that you are going to put mind over matter! You are going to make up in your mind that no matter what the situation looks like you are going to trust God wholeheartedly and you are going to activate your Faith and do it. You woke up renewed this morning. Let's use it!! Let's take full advantage of this second chance to do what we set out to do!! JUST DO IT!! Let's Goooo!! Let's start this week off on fire!!
I pray your day be filled with peace, love, joy, and strength!

*Monday:*_____

How are you going to apply this message in your life today?

_____
_____
_____
_____
_____
_____
_____
_____
_____
_____
_____
_____
_____
_____
_____
_____
_____

Happy Tuesday!!

Today is "Love Yourself Tuesday" When you love yourself first, you attract a different type of "people". Your new vibes are not going to connect with your old vibes. Some people are not going to understand, some people are not going to care, and the ones that really know you and really love you for you, will grow and change with you. You are going to be called conceited, they are going to even say, "who do you think you are?" Your response is always, "no I am not conceited, I am confident in who I am." And to answer the last question, just simply say, "I am *(your name)*, that's who I am, who are you? 90% of the time, those same people that has so much to say about your growth, does not even know who you really are. They are making an assumption. Love yourself in every single area of your life. Love your ups and love your downs. Just do not stay down, but remember those down times are the times you are down in the trenches going through the process. We all have to go through the process to get to our promise!! So love the process, it is only strengthening you. Just think, life is like riding on a plane, you are going to leave the ground and elevate, elevate, elevate until you reach your altitude and then things are going to smooth out. But during that elevation, you are going to hit some turbulence along the way, but you still make it to your smooth elevation.

As God elevate you, some people are not going to be able to breathe at your new altitude. Remember those same people are still on the ground because they can not go where you are going. So let them talk. Remember they look up at you. So, I said all that to say Love YOURSELF first, and it is perfectly ok to outgrow people. You are an eagle, you soar high in the sky, there is a reason the crows, the buzzards, and the pigeons are still flying low and chirping. They will never reach your altitude!! Trust God, Trust the process, and Love yourself!

Tuesday: _____

How are you going to apply this message in your life today?

_____
_____
_____
_____
_____
_____
_____
_____
_____
_____
_____
_____
_____
_____

Happy Wednesday!!

Today is "Direct It Wednesday" As I always say, you wake up every morning with new Grace, new Mercy, and New Life!! Let's treat your life like a movie and you are the Director!! You wake up every day with the chance to dictate your day. You can choose to have a good day, or you can choose to have a not-so-good day. Sometimes life may hit you in the face really hard that day. On those days that's when you put on your directors' hat and you take charge!! You make the choice to redirect the movie. You have the power to change any and everything exactly how you want it to go. Now as a director, you can not do it all alone. You have a team. Your team is your family and friends! Sometimes when we are in director mode, we do not want to listen or take advice from others because it is our life and you are in charge right? Wrong!!

Everyone needs someone on their team to lift them up when they're down, to tell them when they are wrong, to help guide them when the movie is not quite going the way they planned, or someone walked out. Life can sometimes be just like a movie set. But we are going to choose today to be the director of our life. We're going to control the choices we make.

Today we are going to choose to have a great day no matter what. Sometimes even the director has to take a moment and walk off the set, get it together, come back, and try it again. Just like us in our day to day lives, we may be in a situation and we must walk off, take a deep breath, clear our head, and come back! As the director we can not quit! We must keep going no matter what because people are watching. Do not make a permanent decision in a temporary situation. Always look past the moment. When you look past the moment, you will sometimes realize it is not really that serious. So today, I challenge you to take charge of your day. You be the director and direct it well!! I pray you have a fabulous Wednesday!

Wednesday:_____

How are you going to apply this message in your life today?

_____
_____
_____
_____
_____
_____
_____
_____
_____
_____
_____
_____
_____
_____
_____
_____

Happy Thursday!!

Today is "Make a Difference Thursday." Today, I challenge you to not only make a difference in your own life or your immediate loved one's life; today I challenge you to make a difference in a strangers' life. Sometimes that can be a simple smile and saying hello, sometimes that can be as simple as saying "thank you and have a great day." Even when we are going through our situations and pain, being kind to others somehow makes us feel good as well! I know it does for me. We may have an idea of what our love ones or friends may be going through but when you step out and be kind to a perfect stranger, it is completely different. Your gentleness, your kind words, and your words of encouragement may just save someone's life, or it may give that person that final boost they needed to pursue their dreams. So today we are going to be kind and gentle and make a difference in someone else's life. We are going to do it on purpose! So my words to you today are: YOU are amazing, YOU are loved, YOU have the courage, the strength, the knowledge, and the power to do whatever it is you want to do, YOU are strong, YOU are a champion, YOU are beautiful, YOU are blessed, and I LOVE YOU!! Embrace Kindness!! Embrace Love!! And give it to as many others as you can!!

*Thursday:*_____

How are you going to apply this message in your life today?

_____
_____
_____
_____
_____
_____
_____
_____
_____
_____
_____
_____
_____
_____
_____
_____
_____
_____

Happy Friday!!

Yay, you made it to the end of another week!! Today is "ME-DAY Friday." Today you are going to make it your priority to enjoy the day! No matter how your morning began, no matter what news you woke up to. You are going to make up your mind that you are going to celebrate YOU today!! You were blessed to make it through another week. You woke up in your right mind, you still have your vision, you still have your functioning limbs, you still have all your senses, even if you do not have it all, you are alive and breathing and that is all that matters. Be grateful and give thanks for those things we seem to take advantage of daily. So today, I challenge you to have fun. Laugh, dance, joke around, and sing. You spent this entire week working hard, giving your all to your kids, your friends, your family, and others! What about you? Today, you are going to make this day all about you!! Today you declare, "my day will be filled with love, laughter, joy, and happiness!!" Yesterday was about others, today is all about you!! It is not selfish, it is self-care. You must take care of yourself and refill yourself in order to pour into others. You cannot pour anything from an empty cup. Treat yourself to lunch at your favorite spot, treat yourself to that snack that makes you happy and wiggles your toes, and treat yourself to a long nice nap that you want to take but you can not because you are too busy making everyone else a priority.

Friday:_____

How are you going to apply this message in your life today?

_____

_____

_____

_____

_____

_____

_____

_____

_____

_____

_____

_____

_____

_____

_____

_____

Grateful Saturday

List 5 things you are grateful for & why.

1

2

3

4

5

Sunday

List 5 acts of kindness that you will purposely do for someone this week.

1

2

3

4

5

Happy Monday!!

Today is "Keep Hope Monday." The word hope means a desire accompanied by expectation of or belief in fulfillment. Today we are going to be hopeful of our dreams and desires. We are going to be hopeful with great expectations. We are going to hope, trust, and believe in God! We all say we have Faith, but when we pray and ask God for something and it does not seem to go our way, we lose hope, we lose faith, we lose heart and give up. Today, I challenge you to pray with great expectation, pray with your expectations so high that you know only God can fulfill your desires. Your expectations of God's goodness are so high that even when the enemy tries to flash you with the "what if's" and the "what now" you have enough faith in God and enough hope in your heart to keep trusting and keep pushing no matter what! Let's not lose heart! Let's keep our hope alive!! God will give you the desires of your heart if you trust him. "Delight yourself also in the LORD, and He shall give you the desires of your heart."

Psalms 37:4 NKJV. I pray your day be filled with peace, love, and joy. I pray that God gives you ALL the desires of your heart.

56

Monday: _____

How are you going to apply this message in your life today?

_____

_____

_____

_____

_____

_____

_____

_____

_____

_____

_____

_____

_____

_____

_____

_____

_____

_____

Happy Tuesday!!

Today is "Believe in Yourself Tuesday" Even in your darkest days and your darkest hours, there is still hope. The power lies within! With Christ, you have the power to change any circumstance or situation. There is always hope! Dig deep within and pull up the strength that you have buried inside of you! Think back on a time you were in a situation where you thought it was no end in sight!! Now fast forward to now, right now, this very moment, and take a good look at yourself! You made it through, you made it out. So today, I challenge you to dig deep within and rise to that situation! Take your strength back, take your courage back, take your fight back, take your faith back, and charge that thing with force! If God is for you, who can stand against you!! NOBODY!! You are a child of the Highest! Hold your head high, put your shoulders back, stick your chest out, and take this day on like a fierce warrior!!
YOU ARE A CHAMPION!! YOU WILL WIN!!

Tuesday:_____

How are you going to apply this message in your life today?

_____
_____
_____
_____
_____
_____
_____
_____
_____
_____
_____
_____
_____
_____
_____
_____
_____
_____
_____

Happy Wednesday!!

Today is "Joyful Wednesday" Today be joyful, do not just be happy! See, happiness is a feeling that can come and go at any moment, but joy comes from within. The dictionary's definition of happiness and joy pretty much says the same thing, but oooh when I tell you they are way different. Joy runs deep! We turn happiness on and off like a light switch, but joy comes from the Lord!! You must not allow someone to steal your joy! Do not ever lose your joy or give someone that kind of power to take your joy!! See, when you have joy and favor, you have a double dose and no circumstance or situation in hell can steal your joy! It may make you bend a little, but the joy of the Lord and His Favor keeps you from breaking!! But it is during those not-so-good times we have to remember who we are and whose we are!! See, we are children of the Most High. We are made just a little lower than the angels and we are crowned with glory and honor. So today, I challenge you to wear your joy, wear your favor. It does not matter how your day started off, you have the ability and the power to change it. I pray your day be filled with peace, love, and great joy!!

Wednesday:_____

How are you going to apply this message in your life today?

_____
_____
_____
_____
_____
_____
_____
_____
_____
_____
_____
_____
_____
_____
_____
_____
_____
_____

Happy Thursday!!

Today is "Clean up Thursday." Today, we are going to cleanse around us! Sometimes when things are out of order and in disarray, we can not focus or think clearly. That goes for every area. When your house is out of order, you tend to get frustrated and do not even know why. When your desk is messy, you can not seem to focus on your task. When you have people around you that is messy, gossipy and always complaining about something, you can't focus on your tasks, dreams, and goals. We sometimes take on other people's problems and we do not even realize it. We plant ourselves right in the midst of it out of compassion and love. See, messy things and negative people can disturb your peace and before you know it, you are a mess too, and trying to figure out how you got there. It can be very tiring and overwhelming. But today, I challenge you to start cleaning in every area. Just a little at a time and watch how your peace, your energy, and your drive began to be restored! I pray your day is filled with love, peace, and joy. I pray favor over your life. I pray that everything you touch and breathe on has Favor with God and with man!

Thursday:_____

How are you going to apply this message in your life today?

_____
_____
_____
_____
_____
_____
_____
_____
_____
_____
_____
_____
_____
_____
_____
_____
_____
_____
_____

Happy Friday!!

Today is "Fab Friday" Today you are going to have a FABULOUS DAY! You are going to see the good in every single thing that comes your way today. Your day is what you make it!! Choose to have a great day regardless if that coworker upset you this morning. Be thankful you have the job. There are thousands still unemployed and looking for a job, but you have one. Choose to have a great day regardless if your children, spouse, or significant other made you mad this morning. Be thankful they are still alive and healthy. There are thousands of people alone in this world who wish they had family or someone to love them, but you do. Choose happiness regardless!! You choose to have a Fabulous Friday!!! Today is all about what you make it out to be!! Get up and put on your best outfit today!! Look good!!! Smell good!! Feel good!! If you have already started your day, get dressed and enjoy the evening!! Do not let this Friday end without making it the best Friday ever!!! Let's go be great and productive today!! Have a FABULOUS FRIDAY and an amazing weekend!!

*Friday:*_____

How are you going to apply this message in your life today?

_____

_____

_____

_____

_____

_____

_____

_____

_____

_____

_____

_____

_____

_____

_____

_____

Grateful Saturday

List 5 things you are grateful for & why.

1	
2	
3	
4	
5	

Sunday

List 5 acts of kindness that you will purposely do for someone this week.

1

2

3

4

5

Happy Monday!!

Today is "My WHY over Fear Monday," We all have different reasons why we want to do something amazing. Whether it is starting a business, finishing school, going back to school, expanding a business, excelling in a sport... or maybe stopping smoking, stop drinking, or gambling... Everyone has something in their life that they want to accomplish or some habit they want to get rid of regardless of age. But we tend to allow fear to stop us from accomplishing those things. We must put our "WHY" in place. We must figure out our WHY. Your WHY will help you to conquer fear and doubt. Your WHY is far greater than yours. Everyone has a different WHY. Some people's WHY may be their children, their parents, their spouses, or significant others. Some people's WHY may be all about themselves. It does not matter!! When you put your WHY first, it doesn't matter what situation comes up, you will defeat it. Today, I challenge you to find your WHY, find your reason!!! You may get a little uncomfortable but that's ok, that's when faith and growth come into play. We must step outside our comfort zone and go through the process to get to the promise. Take action today, when you have fear and doubt, your WHY will drive you!!! When you get weak, your WHY will give you strength!!!

"For God has not given us a spirit of fear, but of power and of love and of a sound mind." II Timothy 1:7 NKJV

"I can do all things through Christ who strengthens me." Philippians 4:13 NKJV

Monday:_____

How are you going to apply this message in your life today?

_____
_____
_____
_____
_____
_____
_____
_____
_____
_____
_____
_____
_____
_____
_____

Happy Tuesday!!

"Today is Talk About It Tuesday," Let's start this week off by dealing with some things we have been holding on too. Some of those things have broken up friendships, broken up relationships, and may have caused some people some unnecessary stress and anxiety. Sometimes things can be as simple as speaking to someone about what's on your mind and getting an understanding can make things so much easier. But in order to do so, you have to sometimes remove yourself, remove your feelings, and speak from your heart and not your emotions. When people speak from their emotions, they are not thinking clearly because it is so clouded by "what that person did or what you think they did or said". Instead, as humans, we have a habit of holding on to things and making assumptions about things. Don't get me wrong, you may have been blatantly done wrong, mistreated, used, or abused! If you're reading this, God brought you through; His Grace and Mercy brought you out!! He gave you the strength to wake up every day and push despite whatever it was that hurt you! Pick yourself up and drive forward with force! So, today I challenge you to reach out and talk about whatever it is that you have been holding on to. Clear it up! Make peace!

Forgive!!! This is NOT for the other person/people. This is for YOU!! For your peace!! Do not drag all of that into this week!! Speak on it and let it go!! We have too much to do!!

Tuesday: _____

How are you going to apply this message in your life today?

_____

_____

_____

_____

_____

_____

_____

_____

_____

_____

_____

_____

_____

_____

Happy Wednesday!!

Today is "Recharge Wednesday." It's hump day!! Middle of the week!! Two more days to go!! Today we're going to take a step back, take a deep breath, recharge our minds, our bodies, and our hearts to push through the rest of this week!! You got this!! Every day you wake up, you are a step closer to your goals. If your week has already been a rough one, I urge you to take about 20-30 minutes to yourself, pray, and meditate!! Take your mind off the situation and focus your mind on a solution. Focus on the goal itself!! We're all going to hit a few bumps and bruises, but that doesn't mean you have to give up! Dig deep within and take that hit, dust yourself, off and keep pushing forward!! So today, recharge! Your mind and body are just like your cell phone, you would not want it to die right? When it gets close, you do whatever you have to do to find a charger to charge your phone. Well, that same concept goes for our minds and body. Take some time today to recharge your mind, your body, and your strength!! Charge yourself back up!! You cannot help anyone else if you are running low and about to die. If some asks to use your phone and it is low, you say, "Nah, I can't, my battery is about to die" Be the same way with your mind and body. Be selfish with it, the same way you're selfish with your phone when it is about to die!!

Say "no, I can't today or no, not right now, give me a few hours or a few days" RECHARGE!!!! Stop!!! Breathe!!! Pray!!! Meditate!!! Read your Word!!! Even if it's only 15 minutes!! Those 15 minutes can change the course of the rest of your year!! You have the Power!! It lies within!! I pray you have a fabulous day!! I pray today that you will find the time to recharge so that you can charge on with strength and power!!

Wednesday:_____

How are you going to apply this message in your life today?

_____
_____
_____
_____
_____
_____
_____
_____
_____
_____
_____
_____
_____
_____
_____
_____
_____

Happy Thursday!!

Today is "Encourage Thursday," Today we are going to take some time to lift and encourage those around us. Today we're going to take 15-20 minutes to speak life into someone else. Speak life into someone else's vision or dream. Let them know they can do it!! Let them know that they're not alone! Let them know the with God, ALL things are possible!! Encourage them to apply for that promotion, encourage them to go speak to the person that is causing them pain, encourage them to apologize to those they have hurt, and forgive those who hurt them. You never know what the next person is really going through underneath that smile or that pretty face or that handsome face! That 15-20 minutes you give listening and encouraging can save someone's life or keep someone from making a bad decision. So today, I encourage you to be that listening ear, be that shoulder, be that person to lift them up and bring them out. Now do not get me wrong, in order to encourage and lift someone else up you have to prayed up and full. You must ask God to guide your heart and your spirit and give you the right words to say. You must be full; you can't be empty trying to encourage someone else because when you're empty and weak, that same person can pull the little energy you have left and leave you for dead and now all of a sudden you need the

encouragement because you just took all of their problems. So, this morning I encourage you to pray and ask God to give you the strength, and the words to be an encourager today!! I pray your day be filled with peace and many many blessings. I pray that God gives you the knowledge, the wisdom, the strength, and the guidance to uplift and encourage others today!

Thursday:_____

How are you going to apply this message in your life today?

_____

_____

_____

_____

_____

_____

_____

_____

_____

_____

_____

_____

_____

_____

_____

_____

Happy Friday!!

Today is "Celebration Friday," Today we're going to celebrate!! We are going to celebrate everything. The good, the bad, and the ugly!!! Of course, we are going to celebrate the good!! But today we are going to celebrate the bad and the ugly as well. If you woke up this morning and you're still breathing and in your right mind, you need to celebrate!! See all the bad and ugly stuff you went through the past months made you stronger!! It made you wiser!! It made you more appreciative and thankful!! There are some people out there that have gone through the same thing, but they did not come out of it. But with God's Grace and Mercy, He brought you out. So, take a really quick glance and look back at the ugly (don't look too long). whether it was health, finances, relationship, job, or school... look at you now!! You made it!!! You may be still feeling some of the effects, but you are better than you were!!! SO, CELEBRATE YOUR VICTORY!!!
Rejoice and be glad!!!

Friday: _____

How are you going to apply this message in your life today?

_____

_____

_____

_____

_____

_____

_____

_____

_____

_____

_____

_____

_____

_____

_____

_____

Grateful Saturday

List 5 things you are grateful for & why.

1

2

3

4

5

Sunday

List 5 acts of kindness that you will purposely do for someone this week.

1

2

3

4

5

Happy Monday!!

Today is "Affirmation Monday" Today we are going to make up our minds to be EVERYTHING God wants us to be!!! Life and death are in the power of the tongue!! So be really careful what you speak about your life!!
Today we are going to speak life!!!

I AM ALIVE, I AM WELL, I AM WHOLE, I AM HEALED, I AM BLESSED, I AM SMART, I AM VICTORIOUS, I AM BEAUTIFUL, I AM LOVED, I AM STRONG, I AM BRAVE, I HAVE NO FEAR, I WILL ELEVATE, I AM PROSPEROUS, I AM A CHAMPION, I WILL WIN, I AM PERFECTLY BALANCED, I AM UNAPOLOGETICALLY WHO GOD CALLED ME TO BE, I AM UNSTOPPABLE.

Today I pray that you make up in your mind that you're going to speak life over yourself and your family!! I pray that your day be filled with peace, love, and joy.

*Monday:*_____

How are you going to apply this message in your life today?

_____

_____

_____

_____

_____

_____

_____

_____

_____

_____

_____

_____

_____

_____

_____

Happy Tuesday!!

Today is "Work Your Faith Tuesday," "For I say, through the grace given to me, to everyone who is among you, not to think of himself more highly than he ought to think, but to think soberly, as God has dealt to each one a measure of faith." Romans 12:3 NKJV. The scripture says everyone is dealt a measure of faith. Some may activate their faith more than others, but we have all been dealt a measure. Today, I challenge you to activate your faith. Put your faith into action and take that leap! There are so many things you have been wanting to do but you have been doubting yourself and dimming the light on your dreams and goals. You have been taking one step forward and started getting cold feet because you can see the bigger picture and all greatness God has in store for you, but you keep thinking in your head that's way too much, that is not for me!! Then someone says something to you about why you cannot do this or that, and you take two steps back. But what God has in store for you goes far past your wildest dream. He is waiting for you to move out of the way and trust Him! Today, we are going to dump that doubt, that fear, that nervousness, that low self-esteem, and that anxiety!!

We are going to rebuke those things in the Mighty Name of Jesus and command them to go!! NOW!! Today, you're going to hold your head high, adjust your crown, straighten your back and take on today with all your Faith and Trust in God!! If God is for you, who can be against you? NOBODY!!! I pray that you activate your faith! Faith without works is dead! God is waiting on you to make the first move so He can open so many more doors for you! I pray your day be filled with love, peace, and joy.

Tuesday:_____

How are you going to apply this message in your life today?

_____

_____

_____

_____

_____

_____

_____

_____

_____

_____

_____

_____

_____

_____

Happy Wednesday!!

Today is "No Pressure Wednesday," Today we are going to make up the minds that we're going to make decisions to do things on our own terms and our own way. We are going to wait, hear from God, and listen to our own spirit. We are not going to be pressured into anything. Whether it is a relationship, moving to a new location, decision on a new job, purchasing a home, starting a business, wearing a certain outfit, wearing your hair a certain way, or purchasing a new car. People, society, and social media will make you think you are behind or that what your doing is not right. Society and social media will have you thinking what you are doing is not good enough or that what you wear is not good enough. But I am here to tell you that, you are right where you are supposed to be and have what you are supposed to have. Sometimes we see other people and say things like, "I was going to do that, or I'm supposed to be doing that" we even say, "how are they striving in it and I can't" or "I wish I had the courage to wear that, but they may say something about it" Do not get discouraged, you never know what God's plan is. He can be allowing that person to go ahead of you so they can make all the mistakes and go through all the stumbling blocks, so you do not make those same mistakes. It will be smooth for you.

Sometimes He allows other people to go ahead of you to give you the motivation and overcome fear. Because if they can do it, you can do it too. Maybe He didn't let you get approved for that house, or that car, or that apartment. Maybe He allowed you to get turned down from that job. Sometimes we want things so bad and when it does not come through, we get upset and discouraged. But I am here to tell you that God has His hands in everything we do. Do not look at that turn down as a failure, look at it as if God is protecting you from something and He has something much better for you. So, do not allow someone to pressure you into something just because someone else is doing it or someone else has it. Wait until you are ready! Wait until you're comfortable! Wait until you hear from God!! Trust me, you'll know when the time is right!!! Everything will align. I pray you have a marvelous Wednesday! I pray that you have the courage, the wisdom, and the strength to do things in your own terms and your own way!

*Wednesday:*_____

How are you going to apply this message in your life today?

_____
_____
_____
_____
_____
_____
_____
_____
_____
_____
_____
_____
_____
_____
_____
_____

Happy Thursday!!

Today is "Thankful Thursday." Today is a friendly reminder to give God thanks for all that He's done for us and all He continues to do! Thank God for waking you up in your right mind! Thank God for giving you knowledge and understanding! Thank God in advance for what He's about to do in your life! Thank God in advance for your new home, your new car, your new job, and your new apartment! Thank God for your family! Thank God for giving you grace and mercy! Thank God for keeping you shielded and protected from any harm and danger! Thank God for His unwavering favor! Thank God for your health and strength! Even if you don't feel good today, thank Him for your healing!

This scripture says: *"But He was wounded for our transgressions, He was bruised for our iniquities; The chastisement for our peace was upon Him, And by His stripes, we are healed." Isaiah 53:5 NKJV*

Thank your family for loving you no matter what! Thank your friends for being there for you! Today,
GIVE THANKS!

*Thursday:*_____

How are you going to apply this message in your life today?

_____
_____
_____
_____
_____
_____
_____
_____
_____
_____
_____
_____
_____
_____
_____
_____
_____
_____

Happy Friday!!

Today is just a simple but powerful word of encouragement! Remember, it doesn't matter how many cloudy days you may have, one thing for certain, and without any doubt; is that the sun will shine again. Storms never ever last forever. Those storms come through bringing: Rain/Flood (doubt, anxiety, depression, & fear), Thunder (loudmouth people trying to tarnish your name & character) Wind (unexpected bills or car troubles) Lightning (sickness or death). No matter how bad that storm may look in the moment, it is going to pass. You put on your whole armor of God, stand fast, stand strong because before you know it, those cloudy days are gone, and the sun will shine again. If you do those things along with trusting and believing in God, you will come through your storm stronger and more powerful than ever before. You will come out so strong and mighty, that no one will even be able to tell you went through anything. One last thing, be very careful who you talk to or who you allow to speak into your storm. Some people can make your storm worse and last longer. If they're not speaking life, don't allow that energy into your space. *"And let us not grow weary while doing good, for in due season we shall reap if we do not lose heart." Galatians 6:9 NKJV*

*Friday:*_____

How are you going to apply this message in your life today?

_____
_____
_____
_____
_____
_____
_____
_____
_____
_____
_____
_____
_____
_____
_____
_____

Grateful Saturday

List 5 things you are grateful for & why.

1

2

3

4

5

Sunday

List 5 acts of kindness that you will purposely do for someone this week.

1

2

3

4

5

Bonus!! "Forgiveness"

Today, we are going to intentionally do everything with purpose. Start with forgiveness. First, we are going to forgive ourselves for the mistakes that we have made and the things we have done to sabotage ourselves from moving forward. Then we are going to forgive the person that hurt us, the person just keeps coming up and you just cannot get over it. It does not matter what it is. Do not even expect a response. Kindly say "I forgive you" and move on. No explanation is needed. Forgiveness is not for them; forgiveness is for you!! Forgiveness gives you a sense of unexplainable peace.

Forgiveness opens doors

for many blessings. Let's not take those grudges, hurt, and pain into the next month, day, or hour. Let us clear our hearts and our minds so we can truly focus on everything God has for us. Do not allow an unforgiving heart to put a damper on ALLLL the Favor and Blessings God has stored up for you. He's waiting for you. Open your heart, forgive, release that pressure, and move into your greatness. Today is the time to unlatch that trailer you have been dragging around. You will drop it today, so you can lighten your load and make your journey a little lighter and easier!!!
LET IT GO!!! SO, YOU CAN SORE!!

Psychologists generally define forgiveness as a conscious, deliberate decision to release feelings of resentment or vengeance towards a person or group who has harmed you, regardless of whether they deserve your forgiveness. Forgiveness does not mean forgetting, nor does it mean condoning or excusing offenses.

"For if you forgive men their trespasses, your heavenly Father will also forgive you. But if you do not forgive men their trespasses, neither will your Father forgive your trespasses." Matthew 6:14-15 NKJV

A note from the author

With today's busy lifestyles and many uncertainties from the world's many distractions, it is easy to get so wrapped up in life and lose focus on what's really important.

This journal is filled with 35 powerful messages that will help you get through your day. It will help bring a peace and calmness back into your life. By the end of this journal, you will have 35 things you are grateful for and 35 acts of kindness that you purposely shown someone else. Let's start your journey today!

CPSIA information can be obtained
at www.ICGtesting.com
Printed in the USA
BVHW010934260323
661080BV00024B/684